A PASSION FOR FRENCH

A PASSION FOR

FRENCH POETRY

with translations and commentaries

Prys Owen

A PASSION FOR FRENCH POETRY

A PASSION FOR FRENCH POETRY

PRYS OWEN
M.A., Ph.D. (London)
Licence ès Lettres (Lille)

Table of Contents

Table of Contents..2
FOREWORD..4
JOACHIM DU BELLAY 1522 - 1560..............................9
PIERRE DE RONSARD 1524 – 1585..............................13
ALPHONSE DE LAMARTINE 1790-1869....................17
ALFRED DE VIGNY 1797-1863......................................20
VICTOR HUGO 1802 – 1885..29
ALFRED DE MUSSET 1810 – 1857...............................43
THÉOPHILE GAUTIER 1811- 1872................................45
LECONTE DE LISLE 1818 – 1894..................................48
CHARLES BAUDELAIRE 1821- 1867...........................50
PAUL VERLAINE   1844 –1896.......................................55
JEAN-ARTHUR RIMBAUD 1854 – 1891........................62
GUILLAUME APPOLLINAIRE 1880 – 1918..................68
ACKNOWLEDGEMENTS...70
ABOUT THE AUTHOR...71

A PASSION FOR FRENCH POETRY

Il pleure dans mon coeur
Comme il pleut sur la ville.

Say it or whisper
Pleure coeur, pleut ville

Words make verse
Comments are mere
Literature

A PASSION FOR FRENCH POETRY

FOREWORD

The number of children continuing to study French for five years has fallen steadily, and so has the number going on to study it to the age of eighteen Even those who obtained GCE A level in the sixth form may have done so without reading any poetry.

I regret this because French poetry has enriched the whole of my long life as a pupil, a teacher, a trainer of teachers and as one of Her Majesty's Inspectors of Schools

However, some adults may profit from this book by reading it on their own or with friends. All the poems date from 1415 to 1915 and are understandable. That is why I have put them together.

Charles d'Orléans	1394 to 1465
Joachim du Bellay	1522 to 1560
Pierre de Ronsard	1524 to 1585
Alphonse de Lamartine	1790 to 1869
Alfred de Vigny	1797 to 1863
Victor Hugo	1802 to 1885
Alfred de Musset	1810 to 1857
Théophile Gautier	1811 to 1872
Leconte de Lisle	1818 to 1894
Charles Baudelaire	1821 to 1867
Paul Verlaine	1844 to 1896
Jean-Arthur Rimbaud	1854 to 1891
Guillaume Apollinaire	1880 to 1918

I am not fond of grouping poets as members of schools of poetry. They are individuals. However, they themselves did band together – the Pléiade in the sixteenth century and, in the nineteenth century, the Cénacle, the Parnassians and the Symbolists. In the swift flowing nineteenth, where do we place Gautier and, of course, Baudelaire? But it's fun to compare the way three poets wrote of the Sunset.

A PASSION FOR FRENCH POETRY

Victor Hugo

>Oh! regardez le ciel! Cent nuages mouvants.
>Sous leurs flots par moments flamboie un pâle éclair,
>Comme si tout à coup quelque géant de l'air
>Tirait son glaive dans les nues.

A hundred moving clouds, under them lightning flashing, as if some giant of the air was drawing his blade in the clouds.

Théophile Gautier.   (He dedicated his to Hugo.)

>Notre Dame, que c'est beau,
>En passant sur le pont de la Tournelle, un soir,
>Je me suis arrêté quelques instants pour voir
>Le soleil se coucher derrière Notre Dame
>Un nuage splendide à l'horizon de flamme.
>Et moi, je regardais toujours.....

Passing the la Tournelle bridge one evening, I stopped a few moments to see the sun setting behind Notre Dame, a splendid cloud on the flaming horizon. And I, I was observing....

.

Paul Verlaine

>Une aube affaiblie
>Verse par les champs
>La méluncholie
>Des soleils couchants.
>La mélancolie
>Berce de doux chants
>Mon coeur qui s'oublie
>Aux soleils couchants.

.

Fading dawn, pouring the melancholy of the setting suns over the fields. Melancholy nursing with sweet songs my heart in forgetfulness at the setting suns.

A PASSION FOR FRENCH POETRY

....

All my life I have had great pleasure from reading aloud (or reciting from memory) the glorious lyric poetry of France. I hope that my pupils and friends have enjoyed them with me. I suppose that it all began when I was introduced to the nineteenth century Romantic poets when I entered the sixth form in 1944 at the age of fifteen. My main concern at that time, of course, was whether I would get into the first teams for cricket and football. Nevertheless I wanted to go to university to study French and our teacher made it clear that he intended us to succeed in our examinations. But he also loved France and its literature and when he read aloud the last two verses of Victor Hugo's "Booz Endormi", it was clear that this was one of his favourite poems.

Suddenly, seventy years later, I have found a new French lyric poet. He is new to me but much older than the poets of the nineteenth century, and also than the Renaissance poets Ronsard and Du Bellay whom I discovered when I was at Southampton University. This poet was born in 1394 and I feel an empathy with him which refreshes me. My favourite poem is one of the saddest that I've read. We in Wales have a word for exile or loss which is deeply moving for us. It is *hiraeth*. Other Celts know all about it - the Scots after the clearances and the Irish after the potato famines. So what was so special about Charles d'Orléans? He was the Duke of Orleans, father of the future Louis X11. Captured at Agincourt in 1415, five years after he had married Princesse Bonne d'Armagnac, he was not released until 1441, by which time his wife had died. No more delay. Read it aloud. Then, if necessary, read the English version. Sometimes I will begin with the English version or with commentary.

> En regardant vers le pais de France
> Un jour m'avint, a Dovre sur la mer,
> Qu'il me souvint de la doulce plaisance

A PASSION FOR FRENCH POETRY

Que souloye oudit pays trouver.

Paix est tresor qu'on ne peut trop loer.
Je hé guerre, point ne la doy prisier
Destourbé m'a long temps, soit tort ou droit
De voir France que mon cueur amer doit

Las! Mort, qui t'a fait si hardie
De prendre la noble Princesse
Qui estoit mon confort, ma vie,
Mon bien, mon plaisir, ma richesse!

Dieu, qu'il la fait bon regarder,
La gracieuse bonne et belle!
Pour les grans biens qui sont en elle,
Chacun est prest de la louer.
Qui se pourroit d'elle lasser?
Tousjours sa beaulté renouvelle.
Dieu, qu'il la fait bon regarder,
La gracieuse, bonne et belle!
Par deça ne dela la mer,
Ne sçay dame ne demoiselle
Qui estoit en tous biens parfais telle;
C'est un songe que d'y penser,
Dieu, qu'il la fait bon regarder!

It goes on with every stanza ending : "En paine, soussy et douleur." - *pain, care and grief.*

Looking towards the land of France
I happened one day in Dover on Sea
To remember the sweet pleasure
That I was wont there to find.

Peace is a pleasure which can't be too much praised.
I hate war and cannot value it at all.
Hindered for long, rightly or wrongly, was I
From seeing France, owed to my embittered heart.

A PASSION FOR FRENCH POETRY

Alas! Death, who was it who made you so bold,
To take the noble Princess
Who was my comfort, my life,
My Godsend, my pleasure, my wealth!

God , how he makes her good to gaze at,
The gracious, good and beautiful!
For all the gifts which are in her,
Everyone hastens to praise her.
Who could tire of her?
Her beauty is always renewed.
God , how he make her good to gaze at,
The gracious, good and beautiful!
This or that side of the sea,
I know no dame nor demoiselle
Who is in every way perfect as she;
It is a dream merely to think of her,
God , how he makes her good to gaze at!

Although I did not know Charles d'Orleans the poet I had met the twenty one year old Duc d'Orleans in Shakespeare's H*enry V*. At first, with his cousin the Dauphin, he is looking forward with confidence to the battle at Agincourt. Later when Henry and his fierce Welsh "countryman" Captain Fluellen are celebrating victory, Charles is crying out (in Shakespeare's words) "Ô Seigneur. Le jour est perdu, tout est perdu!" and adds ruefully in English: "Is this the King we sent to for his ransom?" He has no idea that he himself will be a prisoner of war for twenty six years, by which time his princess wife will have died. No wonder that in his poem he says that peace is beyond praise, and: "I hate war and see no value in it". Words from the heart, lyric poetry.

A teacher is in a difficult position. Some poets and teachers say that he or she should simply read the poem without background information and commentary. But does it, perhaps, help to give background to Charles d'Orléans' *cri de coeur*?

A PASSION FOR FRENCH POETRY

If we go on to our later nineteenth century poets, we will hear Verlaine saying:

> Que ton vers soit la bonne aventure
> Qui va fleurant la menthe et le thym…..
> Et tout le reste est littérature.

Were my lessons on poetry an adventure, light and fresh, or mere literature? When I was teaching in a boys' school on the Welsh border, the lady who was teaching French in the girls' school crossed the road to speak to me one day.

"What have you been up to – telling your sixth formers to read poetry aloud on their own or when having a picnic in the Black Mountains with a girl friend?"

I think the lines were from from Vigny, one of the first Romantics.

> Le crépuscule ami s'endort dans la vallée
> Sur l'herbe d'éméraude et sur l'or du gazon.

The friendly gloaming sleeps in the valley
On the emerald herb and the golden sward.

And also *The heather is thick on my mountain.*
Il est sur ma montagne une épaisse bruyère.

I was assured that the young lady was enchanted by this vision.

JOACHIM DU BELLAY 1522 - 1560

At the University of Southampton I was introduced to the odes and sonnets of Du Bellay and Ronsard. It was the period of the

A PASSION FOR FRENCH POETRY

sixteenth century Renaissance and they had formed the group of poets called *La Pléiade*. They wanted to recapture the glory of Greek and Latin literature while developing the poetic potential of their mother tongue. Du Bellay translated Virgil and wrote Latin poems all his life, but it was he who wrote a *Defense et Illustration de la Langue Francoyse* in 1549. In the same vein, Ronsard locked his door and read the whole of the Iliad in three days.

Joachim du Bellay. What can one say about a poet who constructed a sonnet in which the two quatrains begin with the same four words: "Je ne te conteray …" and goes on to list Boulogne, Venice, Ferrara, Milan, Naples and Florence? Or who begins another sonnet with six lines starting "Je hay". He tells us that he hates the Florentine for his avarice, the man from Geneva for his rare truth, the Venetian for his malice. And the English?

> Je hay l'Anglais mutin, et le brave Ecossais,
> Le traistre Bourgignon, et l'indiscret François,
> Le superbe Espaignol, et l'yvrogne Thudesque…

The English were probably called mutinous because there had been peasant riots, the adjective "brave" for the Scots probably meant "good fellow" rather than courageous, and "superbe" is used in the Latin meaning of "proud". But, of course, all this perfectly constructed rhythmic, rhyming humour is leading up to the final tercet which he sums up with the introductory "Bref…"

> Bref, je hay quelque vice en chasque nation,
> Je hay moymesme encor mon imperfection,
> Mais je hay par sur tout un sçavoir pédantesque.

In short, I hate some vice in each nation,
I hate again my imperfection,
but I hate above all pedantic knowledge.

You will have noticed changes of spelling over the centuries but it is interesting to see that "above all" was then "par" before "surtout".

A PASSION FOR FRENCH POETRY

The Pléiade recommended imitation of the Greeks and Latins rather than just translations. So I decided to follow their advice because I had things in common with Du Bellay. We both came from mild, west facing regions of a European country with fine slate and swift little rivers and we had both been exiled to great capital cities. Du Bellay's uncle was a cardinal and he had to accompany him to Rome. My family moved to London in the middle of the Second World War. He wrote a fine book of poetry called *Les Regrets* and I shared his *hiraeth* – his for Anjou and mine for the Llŷn Peninsula. I could not hope to match his masterful touches. Note how he balances the two six syllable halves of the twelve syllable Alexandrine lines and how, in the last line, the hard "r"s in "air marin" contrast with the gentle Angevine.

> Heureux qui, comme Ulysse, a fait un beau voyage,
> Ou comme cestuy là qui conquit la toison,
> Et puis est retourné, plein d'usage et raison,
> Vivre entre ses parents le reste de son aage!
>
> Quand revoiray-je helas, de mon petit village
> Fumer la cheminée: et en quel saison
> Revoiray-je le clos de ma pauvre maison,
> Qui m'est une province, et beaucoup d'avantage?
>
> Plus me plaist le sejour qu'ont basty mes ayeux,
> Que des palais Romains le front audacieux:
> Plus que le marbre dur me plaist l'ardoise fine,
>
> Plus mon Loyre Gaulois, que le Tybre Latin,
> Plus mon petit Lyré, que le mont Palatin,
> Et plus que l'air marin la doulceur Angevine.

He contrasts *petit* and *pauvre* with *audacieux*. My quarryman grandfather, who also loved poetry, would have understood.

Let's try to imitate, as the Pléiade advised, then we'll not need a word for word translation. It won't be easy because this will

A PASSION FOR FRENCH POETRY

be trying to write twelve syllable Alexandrine lines rather than English pentameters.

Happy indeed is he, who having journeyed far
Or having searched for wealth in some mysterious land,
Returns with wisdom gained and treasures in his hand
To live with kith and kin, where naught his life can mar.

When will I again see, of my dear village small
The chimneys' drifting smoke? When know the happy time
That homeward I will race, far from this foreign clime
And hear in my own tongue, my loved ones' welcoming call?

More pleasures far for me, the home ancestors built
Than London's city proud, such wealth demanding guilt!
And more than marble halls, the fine-split quarried slate.....

More my swift Celtic streams than old Thames sluggish flow,
Egalitarian Wales than where the Blues do row –
And more my people's words than those of "Good and Great".

Another beautifully crafted sonnet by Du Bellay. I have chosen one which illustrates perfectly how much he hated the artificiality and corruption of the Vatican court. It is addressed to his friend Morel.

J'ayme la liberté, et languis en service,
Je n'ayme pas la Court, et me fault courtiser,
Je n'ayme la feintise, et me fault deguiser,
J'ayme simplicité, et n'apprens que malice.

Je n'adore les biens, et sers à l'avarice,
Je n'ayme les honneurs, et me les fault priser,
Je veulx garder ma foy, et me la fault briser,
Je cherche la vertu, et ne trouve que vice.

A PASSION FOR FRENCH POETRY

Je cherche le repos, et trouver ne le puis,
J'embrasse le plaisir, et n'esprouve qu'ennuis,
Je n'ayme à discourir, en raison je me fonde:

J'ay le corps maladif, et me fault voyager,
Je suis né pour la Muse, on me fait mesnager:
Ne suis-je pas (Morel) le plus chetif du monde?

I love liberty and languish in service,
I don't like the Court and I have to act the courtier,
I don't like pretence and and I am forced to act a part,
I like simplicity and only learn malice.

I don't like possessions and serve avarice,
I don't like honours, and I have to value them,
I want to keep my word, and I have to break it,
I seek virtue, and only find vice.

I look for rest, and can't find it,
I love pleasure and only experience tedium,
I don't like discourse, I base myself on reason.

I have a sickly body, and I have to travel,
I was born for the Muse, they make me a manager:
Am I not (Morel) the most wretched man in the world?

PIERRE DE RONSARD 1524 – 1585

Ronsard may have gloried in and recommended the study of Greek and Latin literature but it is his own words which sing of the wonder of love and nature. He shows plenty of humour – teasing Hélène that when she rereads his verses in old age it would be "en

A PASSION FOR FRENCH POETRY

vous esmerveillant". No false modesty here. It is also in a teasing mood that he says to Marie, "Levez-vous".

This first poem is not a sonnet but an ode - a famous one on the old, old theme of *carpe diem*. We are reminded of Shakespeare, and of Herrick's "Gather ye rosebuds while ye may", but they were a whole generation after Ronsard.

> Mignonne, allon voir si la rose
> Qui ce matin avoit desclose
> Sa robe de pourpre au Soleil,
> A point perdu ceste vesprée
> Les plis de sa robe pourprée,
> Et son teint au vostre pareil.
> Las! Voyez comme en peu d'espace
> Mignonne, elle a dessus la place
> Las! Las! ses beautez laissé cheoir!
> O vrayment marastre Nature,
> Puis qu'une telle fleur ne dure
> Que du matin jusques au soir!
> Donc, si vous me croyez, mignonne,
> Tandis que vostre âge fleuronne
> En sa plus verte nouveauté,
> Cueillez, cueillez vostre jeunesse:
>
>
> Comme à ceste fleur la vieillesse
> Fera ternir vostre beauté

"Traduire c'est trahir," but I will risk a translation.

Sweetheart, let us see if the rose
Which did this very morn disclose
Its purple robes to the sun
Has lost at even's sunset gold
Many a fine rich purple fold,
Like your smooth cheeks which hearts have won.
Alas, see how in one short day

A PASSION FOR FRENCH POETRY

My love, it has on that pathway,
Alas, its beauties laid aside.
Oh, truly harsh Mother Nature,
That a flower which you did nurture
Lasts not from morn to eventide!
So believe me, my sweet darling
While your smile is still beguiling,
Using freshness is a duty.
Go, gathering kisses, now be bold.
Like every flower you will grow old
Losing precious youthful beauty.

On the same theme, Ronsard did write sonnets. In this one he rightly boasts of his immortal genius.

Quand vous serez bien vieille, au soir, à la chandelle,
Assise aupres du feu, devidant et filant,
Direz chantant mes vers, en vous esmerveillant:
Ronsard me celebroit du temps que j'estois belle.

Lors vous n'aurez servante oyant telle nouvelle,
Desja sous le labour à demy sommeillant,
Qui au bruit de mon nom ne s'aille resveillant,
Benisssant vostre nom de louange immortelle .

Je seray sous la terre, et fantosme sans os
Par les ombreux myrteux je prendray mon repos:
Vous serez au fouyer une vieille accroupie,

Regrettant mon amour et vostre fier desdain,
Vivez, si m'en croyez, n'attendez à demain:
Cueillez dés aujourd'huy les roses de la vie.

When you're quite old, in evening candlelight,
Snug seated by the fire, slow time sewing to pass,
You will say of my verse, all wondering with delight,
Ronsard 'twas who praised me when then a lovely lass..

A PASSION FOR FRENCH POETRY

Then no servant you'll have, to harken wondrous news,
By her labour fatigued, and almost half asleep,
Who, when hearing my name would remember my muse,
Loudly blessing your name and to compliment leap..

Under sod I shall be, just a ghost newly laid,
In deep purple shadow, to my rest I'll be sent.
You will be at the hearth , an old lady quite bent,

Regretting my loving and your so proud disdain.
Get a life, believe me, wait not for the morrow,
Gather roses today, or then you'll have sorrow.

As always, Du Bellay and Ronsard are masters of the Alexandrine. Read these verses, exaggerating perhaps,the caesura which divides the lines in halves - but retaining the flow.

We will treat ourselves to one more of Ronsard's cheeky verses to a young lady. This time it is to Marie who is lazily staying in bed instead of getting up and doing the gardening. *The lark and the nightingale are cheerfully singing their songs of love. The little pearly shrubs and the beautifully budding rose and the little pinks that you watered so carefully yesterday evening. You swore last night to be up earlier than me, but your eyes are still closed. I will kiss you a hundred times in order to teach you to get up in the morning.* Enjoy these lines bubbling with fun Not Joachim's *Regrets* here.

Marie, levez-vous, vous estes paresseuse,
Ja la gaye alouette au ciel a fredonné,
Et ja le rossignol doucement jargonné,
Dessus l'espine assis, sa complainte amoureuse.

Sus debout, allon voir l'herbelette perleuse,
Et vostre beau rosier de boutons couronné
Et vos oeillets mignons ausquels aviez donné
Hier au soir de l'eau d'une main si songneuse.

A PASSION FOR FRENCH POETRY

    Harsoir en vous couchant vous jurastes vos yeux,
    D'estre plustost que moy ce matin esveillée;
    Mais le dormir de l'aube, aux filles gracieux,

    Vous tient d'un doux sommeil encor les yeux sillées,
    Ça ça que je les baise et vostre beau tetin
    Cent fois pour vous apprendre à vous lever matin.

ALPHONSE DE LAMARTINE 1790-1869

We leap forward from Ronsard's death in 1585 to Lamartine's birth in 1790, He is the first of the Romantic group of poets that we will read. But the themes of nature and love and exotic places like America have already been romantically celebrated in the colourful prose of Chateaubriand.

So many of us started learning French nineteenth century Romantic poetry by learning off by heart and reciting:"O temps suspends ton vol! Et vous, heures propices, Suspendez votre cours!"

The lines are from Lamartine's *Le Lac* and he addresses the lake in the "tu" form. They are old friends. He is returning alone.

    O lac! l'année à peine a fini sa carrière
    Et près des flots chéris qu'elle devait revoir
    Regarde! Je viens seul m'asseoir sur cette pierre
      Où tu la vis s'asseoir.

It was his loved one who had asked time to stand still for those who are happy. Now she has died.

    Aimons donc, aimons donc! de l'heure fugitive,
    Hâtons-nous, jouissons!
    L'homme n'a point de port, ou le temps n'a point de rive;
      Il coule, et nous passons!

A PASSION FOR FRENCH POETRY

Temps jaloux, se peut-il que ces moments d'ivresse,
Où l'amour à longs flots nous verse le bonheur,
S'envolent loin de nous de la même vitesse
   Que les jours de malheur?

Hé quoi! n'en pourrons-nous fixer au moins la trace?
Quoi! passés pour jamais? quoi ! tout entier perdus?
Ce temps qui les donna ce temps qui les efface,
   Ne nous les rendra plus?

This is Romantic poetry of the sentiments. It is a cry from the heart to the reader. The first of these three stanzas is a cry in the first person plural. *Let's hurry, let's enjoy ! Man has no port, time has no limit, it flows and we pass! Jealous time, can it be that these moments of ecstasy when love pours happiness on us, flows far from us with the same speed as days of misfortune?* Then the stanza beginning "He quoi!" goes on with five exclamations in the first two lines. *Can't we even fix some memory? What! Gone for ever? What! All completely lost? This time which gave them, this time which took them away, will it not give them back any more?*

So the poet now calls on nature, the whole of this lakeside, to keep the memory of their love.

O lac! rochers muets! grottes! forêt obscure !
Vous que le temps épargne ou qu'il peut rajeunir,
   Gardez de cette nuit, gardez, belle nature,
      Au moins le souvenir!

You whom time spares or whom it can rejuvenate, guard of this night, guard, beautiful nature, at least the memory!

The final stanza, which I loved romantically at the age of seventeen, still gives pleasure. Do I need to translate?

Que le vent qui gémit, le roseau qui soupire
Que les parfums légers de ton air embaumé

Prys Owen

A PASSION FOR FRENCH POETRY

Que tout ce qu'on entend, l'on voit ou l'on respire,
   Tout dise: "Ils ont aimé."

That the wind which wails, the reed which sighs, that the light perfumes of your scented breeze, that all that one hears, that one sees or that one breathes, all say: "They have loved."

When he is facing death where can he turn? It is to the valley of his childhood, *Le Vallon*

   Prêtez-moi seulement, vallon de mon enfance,
   Un asile d'un jour pour attendre la mort.

   Ah! c'est là qu'entouré d'un rempart de verdure,
   D'un horizon borné qui suffit à mes yeux,
   J'aime à fixer mes pas, et, seul dans la nature
   À n'entendre que l'onde, à ne voir que les cieux.

Give me only, valley of my childhood,
One day's refuge to await death

Ah! It is there that surrounded by a rampart of greenery,
With a limited horizon which is enough for my eyes,
I aim to stay in one place, and, alone in nature,
Only hearing the wave, seeing only the skies

This is the classic Romantic poet alone in nature where, in the words of Jean Jacques Rousseau, "No unwanted third person can come between nature and me." And I remember being told to learn off by heart the next four lines. Here they are without a glance at the book.

   Mais la nature est là qui t'invite et qui t'aime;
   Plonge-toi dans son sein qu'elle t'ouvre toujours:
   Quand tout change pour toi, la nature est la même,
   Et le même soleil se lève sur tes jours.

But nature is there which invites you and loves you;

A PASSION FOR FRENCH POETRY

Plunge into its breast which it opens to you always:
When everything changes for you, nature is the same,
And the same sun rises on your days!

ALFRED DE VIGNY 1797-1863

Vigny was a soldier. He translated *Othello* and *The Merchant of Venice* and he wrote plays and novels. *Cinq Mars* was written in 1826.

Moise and *La Colère de Samson* are, of course, Bible stories but he uses them to convey a wider message. The third story is the story of a wolf hunt. This is used to express a philosophy. Reading these again after many years my enjoyment has increased. I appreciate particularly the way he conveys the weight of responsibility in *Moise* and the frightening drama of *La Mort du Loup*.

Le soleil prolongeait sur la cime des tentes
Ces obliques rayons, ces flammes éclatantes,
Ces larges traces d'or qu'il laisse dans les airs,
Lorsqu'en un lit de sable il se couche aux déserts.
La pourpre et l'or semblait revêtir la campagne.

The reader feels immediately that the poet knows the desert which he describes, with the weight of the rhyming Alexandrines. Sterile Nebo conveys local colour which he adds to later with Galaad, Éphraim and Manassé. The scene set, we are introduced to Vigny's Moses. Instead of naming him at the beginning of the sentence, he is described climbing up the mountain, stopping and studying the scene with authority.

Du stérile Nebo gravissant la montagne,
Moise, l'homme de Dieu, s'arrête, et, sans orgueil,
Sur le vaste horizon promène un long coup d'oeil.

A PASSION FOR FRENCH POETRY

We are gripped by the story immediately. We feel that we know Moses - yes ,the man of God but a leader of thousands of men. How does Vigny convey how much he takes in with a mere glance? And he emphasises it immediately with "ses regards parcourent." He contrasts the desert with the plains.

> Plus loin, dans un vallon que le soir a pali,
> Couronné d'oliviers, se montre Nephtali;
> Dans des plaines de fleurs magnifiques et calmes,
> Jéricho s'aperçoit: c'est la ville de palmes;

Stop now and please read aloud, with contrast in tone and volume, these two quotations.

The story moves on and we get a first hint of why this is a tragedy. But before we read these key last lines of the first section, I must try a translation of what we have read in case you have had some difficulties.

*The sun extended on to the tops of the tents these oblique rays, these glaring flames, these wide trails of gold which it leaves in the air, when into a bed of sand it descends in the deserts. (*Not singular but plural. He is not just describing what he is seeing, but also what Moses knows.*) The purple and gold seemed to clothe the landscape. From sterile Nebo, scaling the mountain, Moses, man of God, stops and without pride, over the vast horizon extends a long glance. Further on, in a valley paling at eventide, crowned with olives, Nephtali is seen; in plains of magnificent calm flowers Jericho appears; it is the town of palm trees.*

Now Moses sees Canaan and the Promised Land, but deep down he realises that he will not be allowed to have his tomb there. He sees; over the Hebrews he stretches his great hand, then towards the top of the mountain he restarts his climb.

> Il voit tout Chanaan et la terre promise,
> Où sa tombe, il le sait, ne sera point admise.
> Il voit; sur les Hébreux étend sa grande main,

A PASSION FOR FRENCH POETRY

Puis vers le haut du mont il reprend son chemin.

The children of Israel were in the valley like blades of wheat moving in the wind, agitated because they realized that great drama was unfolding.

Les enfants d'Israel s'agitaient au vallon
Comme les blés épais qu'agite l'aquilon.
Prophète centenaire, environné d'honneur,
Moïse était parti pour trouver le Seigneur

As his flock below are singing hymns to the King of Kings, Moses is standing before God . He is not on his knees in that dark cloud.

Et debout devant Dieu, Moïse ayant pris place,
Dans le nuage obscur lui parlait fâce à fâce.
Il disait au Seigneur: "Ne finirai-je pas?
Où voulez-vous encore que je porte mes pas?
Je vivrai donc toujours puissant et solitaire?
Laissez-moi m'endormir du sommeil de la terre!

The great leader asks three questions and ends with an exclamation. Note the question which, bowed down with responsibility, he asks. It will be echoed in the thoughts of his successor as the poem ends. Vigny wrote *Servitudes et Grandeurs Militaires* and understood these matters. I have led men!

Que vous ai-je donc fait pour être votre élu?
J'ai conduit votre peuple où vous avez voulu.

Over four more powerful sections Moses repeats to God what his power has represented . Even the angels have been jealous when he calmed seas.

Et cependant, Seigneur, je ne suis pas heureux;
Vous m'avez fait vieillir puissant et solitaire,
Laissez-moi m'endormir du sommeil de la terre!

A PASSION FOR FRENCH POETRY

This is repeated once more until the mountain top becomes visible again and there is no sign of Moses. He was mourned, but another must take over.

> Josué s'avançait pensif et pâlissant,
> Car il était déjà l'élu du Tout-Puissant.

La Maison du Berger

Can nature be for Vigny what it was for Lamartine and for most of the Romantics? The first four stanzas start in the same way. If your heart is groaning with the weight of your life, if your soul is in chains, as mine is - if it is looking for beauty ...

"Pars courageusement, laisse toutes les villes ….J'y roulerai pour toi la Maison du Berger." The shepherd's caravan on four wheels. But no. What does nature say?

> Elle me dit, "Je suis l'impassible théâtre
> Que ne peut remuer le pied de ses acteurs;…
> Je n'entends ni vos cris ni vos soupirs; à peine
> Je sens passer sur moi la comédie humaine..

> *She says to me "I am the unfeeling theatre*
> *Which the feet of her actors cannot stir…*
> *I do not hear your cries or your sighs; hardly*
> *Do I feel passing over me the human comedy.*

So this poet says that man may suffer but he is superior to "la froide nature,".

> L'homme, humble passager, qui dut vous être un Roi;

A PASSION FOR FRENCH POETRY

Plus que tout votre règne et que ses splendeurs vaines
J'aime la majesté des souffrances humaines:
Vous ne recevrez pas un cri d'amour de moi.

Man, humble passenger, who should be a King to you;
More than all your reign and all its vain splendour
I love the majesty of human suffering:
You will not receive a cry of love from me.

La Colère de Samson

    I used to be quite scornful about this poem. Vigny wrote it after his actress mistress had betrayed him. First he sets the scene with local colour and introduces the characters:

Une lutte éternelle en tout temps, en tout lieu,
Se livre sur la terre, en présence de Dieu,
Entre la bonté d'Homme et la ruse de Femme,
Car la femme est un être impur de corps et d'âme.

    We are told by the poet that this is a sad funereal chant in Hebrew that Samson's slave Dalila does not understand. So one might say that neither the poet nor Samson are fully responsible!

*   An eternal struggle in all times, everywhere, is waged on earth, in the presence of God, between the goodness of Man and the wile of Woman, because woman is an impure being in body and soul.*

L'Homme a toujours besoin de caresse et d'amour,
Sa mère l'en abreuve alors qu'il vient au jour.

A PASSION FOR FRENCH POETRY

Man has always needed to be caressed and loved. His mother has so provided him from when he saw the light of day.

In a lonely tent in the desert when "la nuit n'a pas calmé la fournaise du jour," we are introduced to the great young master, Samson, who by "divine force" obeys his slave, and Dalila. who is described exotically:

> Comme un doux léopard elle est souple, et répand
> Ces cheveux dénoués aux pieds de son amant.
> Ses grands yeux entr'ouverts comme s'ouvre l'amande,
> Sont brûlants du plaisir que son regard demande.

Like a gentle leopard she is supple and spreads her loosened hair at the feet of her lover. Her wide eyes half opened as an almond opens, are burning with the pleasure which her glance demands.

Of course, God gets the blame, forcing Man to the kiss which he needs. Samson, in addition to his battles with the warriors of the false god Dagon, has to face the cowardly treachery of Dalila, betraying the secret that Samson's strength will be lost if his hair is cut. "La Femme est toujours Dalila."

> Elle se fait aimer sans aimer elle-même;
> Un maître lui fait peur. C'est le plaisir qu'elle aime.

She makes herself loved without feeling love herself. But despite being blinded through her treachery Samson manages to shake the columns of the temple, and three thousand enemies are destroyed. Treason is punished. A secret had been betrayed "par des baisers menteurs."

La Mort du Loup is not a Bible story but the scene is set in the same way before the action starts. Yet there is a difference. True, the first line has the usual Romantic drama:

> Les nuages couraient sur la lune enflammée

A PASSION FOR FRENCH POETRY

Comme sur l'incendie on voit fuir la fumée,
Et les bois étaient noirs jusques à l'horizon.

The clouds ran across the flaming moon, as we see smoke flying across the fire. The woods were black as far as the horizon.

Then everything changes. Action, and the storyteller is personally involved, tense and silent. "Nous marchions sans parler…" Under the pines they find the paw prints of the wolves they have been tracking. We are only at the eighth line. This is quite different from Moses and Samson. Vigny brilliantly conveys tension.

Nous avons écouté, retenant notre haleine
Et le pas suspendu - Ni le bois ni la plaine
Ne poussaient un soupir dans les airs; seulement
La girouette en deuil criait au firmament.

How I wish that I'd composed those lines! Read them aloud either to yourself or to a friend who is also, perhaps, rediscovering a love of France and her poetry.

We listened, holding our breath, and halted mid step. (I can see the hunters like tigers, one foot suspended in the air). The caesura after the suspendu and then the *enjambement,* so that "ne poussaient" carries on the flow from the two subjects, is very effective. Only the bird in grief cried to the sky. The team of hunters are depending on the oldest hunter, who never made a mistake, and now:

A déclaré tout bas que ces marques récentes
Annonçaient la démarche et les griffes puissantes
De deux grands loups-cerviers et de deux louveteaux.

He whispers that the recent tracks are of two adult lynx and their cubs. Everything happens quickly, though quietly. (couteaux préparés, fusils cachés) and then suddenly:

A PASSION FOR FRENCH POETRY

> Trois s'arrêtent, et moi, cherchant ce qu'ils voyaient,
> J'aperçois tout à coup deux yeux qui flamboyaient,

Two present tenses. Why? And without a full stop after the flaming eyes , we have -

> Et je vois au delà quatre formes légères
> Qui dansaient sous la lune au milieu des bruyères,
> Comme font chaque jour, à grand bruit, sous nos yeux,
> Quand le maître revient, les lévriers joyeux.
> Leur forme était semblable, et semblable la danse;

Note the light, musical, dancing character of these lines. *And I see over there four light shapes, dancing under the moon among the heathers, as do every day, noisily, before our eyes, when the master returns, the joyous greyhounds. Their form was similar, and similar the dance;*

But the next line is almost brutally not dancing."Mais les enfants du Loup jouaient en silence." We need no explanation. The next four lines concentrate on the mother. How does the poet claim particular sympathy for her?

> Le père était debout, et plus loin, contre un arbre
> Sa louve reposait comme celle de marbre
> Qu'adoraient les Romains et dont les flancs velus
> Couvaient les demi-dieux Rémus et Romulus.

The father was standing, and further away, against a tree his she-wolf rested like the one in marble whom the Romans adored and whose velvet flanks......("hairy" seems inappropriate*) suckled the semi-gods Remus and Romulus.*

The wolf has been surprised and knows that he has lost..... but there are three sections to the story and we are only three quarters of the way through the first section. Is the hunt almost over? If so, what is the rest about? The wolf has been shot and the hunters' knives have been plunged into his entrails.

Prys Owen

A PASSION FOR FRENCH POETRY

> Alors il a saisi, dans sa gueule brûlante,
> Du chien le plus hardi la gorge pantelante
> Et n'a pas desserré ses mâchoires de fer,
> Malgré nos coups de feu qui traversaient sa chair.

This is powerful stuff. Notice how he reverses the second line to get the two rhyming key words "brûlante" and "pantelante." The hard consonants in "desserré, mâchoires, fer" stress the ferocity of battle. Now the emphasis is entirely on the manner of the wolf's death..

> Il nous regarde encore, ensuite il se recouche,
> Tout en léchant le sang répandu sur sa bouche,
> Et, sans daigner savoir comment il a péri,
> Refermant ses grands yeux, meurt sans jeter un cri.

In the previous stanza the wolf's jaw was "sa gueule brûlante," now the blood is on his mouth. Is the poet giving him human dignity?

Then he seizes in his burning jaw the panting neck of the most daring dog and does not loosen his iron teeth despite our shots which penetrate his flesh. He looks at us again, then lies down, licking the blood spread on his mouth, and without deigning to know how he perished, closing his great eyes, dies without uttering a cry.

Section Two concerns the immediate reaction of the poet/storyteller. He rests his head on his gun - "me prenant à penser". He is about to philosophise. What is the moral of this experience? Firstly, he found he could not carry on hunting the wolf's family. Secondly, the mother knew that her duty was to teach her cubs to tolerate hunger but to remain with the glory of being wild animals.

> À ne jamais entrer dans le pacte des villes
> Que l'homme a fait avec les animaux serviles
> Qui chassent devant lui, pour avoir le coucher,
> Les premiers possesseurs du bois et du rocher.

A PASSION FOR FRENCH POETRY

Never to enter the pact of the towns that man has made with the servile animals, who hunt in front of him, in order to have their bread and board though they were the first owners of the woods and the rocks.

Hélas! ai-je pensé, malgré ce grand nom d'Hommes,
Que j'ai honte de nous, débiles que nous sommes!
Comment on doit quitter la vie et tous ses maux,
C'est vous qui le savez, sublimes animaux!

Alas! I thought, despite this great name of Men, how ashamed I am of us, weak that we are. How one should leave life and all its evils, it's you who know, sublime animals.. He talks of their stoic pride. This is the philosophy he advocates.

Gémir, pleurer, prier, est également lâche.
Fais énergiquement ta longue et lourde tâche
Dans la voie où le Sort a voulu t'appeler.
Puis après, comme moi, souffre et meurs sans parler.

This is the soldier/poet speaking in measured and dignified language. *Moaning, crying, praying are equally cowardly. Perform energetically your long and heavy task in the way that Fate has chosen to call you. Then afterwards, like me, suffer and die without speaking.*

VICTOR HUGO 1802 – 1885

Some poets we leave with a smile of pleasure.. We leave Vigny, particularly after reading *La Mort du Loup*, feeling deeply moved and swept along by the dignity of his verses. But now we turn to the master. Hugo is a colossus and was respected as a leader by his fellow poets in the nineteenth century. Of course he was a dramatist and a novelist as well as a poet. Apart from a break when he was heavily involved in politics, he wrote to the end of his eighty three years. Which of his poems to read? We will follow Vigny with an

A PASSION FOR FRENCH POETRY

epic poem in the same vein, *L'Expiation*. After he had died, what was going to be God's punishment for Napoleon's ambition? Was it to be shown his retreat from Moscow? I wonder if Hitler ever read this poem? He made exactly the same mistake as Napoleon. Both experienced in their retreats from Moscow "Après la plaine blanche une autre plaine blanche."

> Il neigeait. On était vaincu par sa conquête.
> Pour la première fois l'aigle baissait la tête.
> Sombres jours! L'empereur revenait lentement,
> Laissant derrière lui brûler Moscou fumant
> Il neigeait. L'âpre hiver fondait en avalanche..
> Après la plaine blanche une autre plaine blanche.
> On ne connaissait plus les chefs ni le drapeau.
> Hier la grande armée, et maintenant troupeau .
> On ne distinguait plus les ailes ni le centre.
> Il neigeait. Les blessés s'abritaient dans le ventre
> Des chevaux morts ……..
> Boulets, mitraille, obus, mêlés aux flocons blancs

It was snowing. Conquest had led to defeat. For the first time the eagle lowered its head. Sombre days! The emperor retreated slowly, leaving behind him Moscow in flame and smoke. It was snowing. The harsh winter was melting into an avalanche. And then the apparently simple repetition: *After the white plain another white plain.* But in French the repeated vowels convey the never ending snow. *No longer were the commanders or the flag recognized. Yesterday the great army, and now a herd* (note that is not "troupe" but "troupeau" - a herd). *Bullets, grape shot, shells, mingling with the white flakes rained down.* Has anyone ever given a better description of winter warfare?

Then we have the repeated: "Il neigeait, il neigeait toujours." *What was the sun but a white shroud over the dead.*

> Pour cette immense armée un immense linceul,
> Et chacun se sentait mourir, on était seul.

A PASSION FOR FRENCH POETRY

Here a startling contrast between "immense armee" and each man dying alone. "On s'endormait dix mille, on se réveillait cent." *Ten thousand went to sleep, a hundred awoke. A whole army in the night was lost like this. The emperor was standing there, looking.* "Toute une armee ainsi dans la nuit se perdait.L'empereur était là, debout, regardait."

And so, when facing God after his death, Napoleon asks: "Est-ce le châtiment, dit-il, Dieu des armées?" Non.

Then comes the second part of the Atonement. Waterloo.

Waterloo! Waterloo! Waterloo! Morne plaine!
Comme une onde qui bout dans une urne trop pleine
Like a wave boiling in an over full jar.

D'un côté c'est l'Europe et de l'autre la France.

Then when it seemed that reinforcements were coming in the form of Grouchy, they were for Wellington. Blucher. We feel the change of fortune after three words of sudden hope. "Soudain, joyeux, il dit: Grouchy! – C'était Blucher."

Moi vaincu! Mon empire est brisé comme verre.
Est-ce le châtiment cette fois, Dieu sévère?
Alors parmi les cris, les rumeurs, le canon,
Il entendit la voix qui répondait: Non!

So Napoleon goes into exile.

Adieu le cheval blanc que César éperonne!
Plus de tambours battant aux champs, plus de couronne.
Seigneur! C'est maintenant fini! Dieu que j'implore,
Vous m'avez châtié! - La voix dit:- Pas encore," *Not yet.*

Hugo enjoyed the thought of himself as a grandfather. He wrote *L'art d'être grand'pere*. Nothing could be further from warfare than: *Lorsque l'enfant paraît.*

A PASSION FOR FRENCH POETRY

> Lorsque l'enfant paraît, le cercle de famille
> Applaudit à grands cris.Son doux regard qui brille
>   Fait briller tous les yeux,
> Et les plus tristes fronts, les plus souillés peut-être,
> Se dérident soudain à voir l'enfant paraître,
>   Innocent et joyeux.

The weight of the twelve syllable Alexandrine couplets is replaced by two short lines which sum up the message. *The child makes all eyes shine, he is innocent and joyous. And the saddest faces, the most soiled, perhaps, suddenly stop frowning, seeing the child appear, innocent and joyful.* We note little touches which show Hugo's familiarity with the situation. "Sa mère tremble à le voir marcher." Not only pride but fear that he will fall. We can picture her half stepping forward with arms outstretched. Everyone is affected, even the poets, says Hugo , with a wink of the eye.

> Quelquefois nous parlons, en remuant la flamme,
> De patrie et de Dieu, des poètes, de l'âme
>   Qui s'élève en priant;
> L'enfant paraît, adieu le ciel et la patrie
> Et les poètes saints! La grave causerie
>   S'arrête en souriant.

There are smiles everywhere and again even discussion of the sacred poets stops. Of course, there is more than a touch of idealism here, and indeed we recall Jean-Jacques Rousseau.

> Car vos beaux yeux sont pleins de douceurs infinies,
> Car vos petites mains, joyeuses et bénies,
>   N'ont point mal fait encore;
> Jamais vos jeunes pas n'ont touché notre fange,
> Tête sacrée! enfant aux cheveux blonds! bel ange
>   À l'auréole d'or!

Your little, blessed hands have not yet done wrong, never have your young feet touched our filth. Wordsworth also said that

A PASSION FOR FRENCH POETRY

the child comes trailing clouds of glory. Hugo stresses the sacred head of this beautiful angel.

The grandfather not only knows about the beauty of children and their sweet smile but also about their trusting nature, their voice which wants to say everything, the tears which disappear as suddenly as they arrive. They are astonished and delighted with all the new things which they see, offering their young soul to life, and their lips to kisses.

> Il est si beau , l'enfant, avec son beau sourire,
> Sa douce bonne foi, sa voix qui veut tout dire,
>   Ses pleurs vite apaisés,
> Laissant errer sa vue étonnée et ravie,
> Offrant de toutes parts sa jeune âme à la vie
>   Et sa bouche aux baisers!

The final stanza is a masterpiece. The speeding enumerations give it a powerful rhythmic beat. Perhaps our modern sensitivities (unless we keep canaries) may baulk at the glorification of the bird cage. Note also that his enemies triumph in evil while he calls twice on the Lord.

> Seigneur! préservez-moi, préservez ceux que j'aime,
> Frères, parents, amis, et mes ennemis même
>   Dans le mal triomphants,
> De jamais voir, Seigneur, l'été sans fleurs vermeilles,
> La cage sans oiseaux, la ruche sans abeilles,
>   La maison sans enfants!

> *Lord! preserve me, preserve those whom I love,*
> *Brothers, kinsmen, friends, and even my enemies*
>   *In evil triumphant,*
> *From ever seeing, Lord, summer without vermilion f*
> *flowers,*
> *The cage without birds, the hive without bees,*

A PASSION FOR FRENCH POETRY

The house without children!

I am choosing three more poems by Hugo - firstly a short one of three stanzas to which I shall wish to refer again when we read one of Rimbaud's poems. Then a few stanzas from a very sad poem. And finally one which ends with two of my favourite stanzas.

Demain, dès l'aube…..*Tomorrow, at dawn….*

> Demain, dès l'aube, à l'heure où blanchit la campagne,
> Je partirai. Vois-tu, je sais que tu m'attends.
> J'irai par la forêt, j'irai par la montagne.
> Je ne puis demeurer loin de toi plus longtemps.
>
> Je marcherai les yeux fixés sur mes pensées,
> Sans rien au dehors, sans entendre aucun bruit,
> Seul, inconnu, le dos courbé, les mains croisées,
> Triste, et le jour pour moi sera comme la nuit.
>
> Je ne regarderai ni l'or du soir qui tombe,
> Ni les voiles au loin descendant vers Harfleur,
> Et quand j'arriverai, je mettrai sur ta tombe
> Un bouquet de houx vert et de bruyère en fleur.

> *Tomorrow, at dawn, when the countryside is whitening,*
> *I will set off. You see, I know that you are waiting for me.*
> *I will go through the forest, I will go by the mountain.*
> *I can't stay without you any longer.*
>
> *I will walk with my eyes fixed on my thoughts,*
> *Seeing nothing about me, not hearing any sound,*
> *Alone, unknown, back bent, hands clasped together,*
> *Sad, and the day for me will be like night.*
>
> *I will not look at the gold of falling eventide,*
> *Nor the distant sails descending towards Harfleur,*
> *And when I arrive, I will place on your tomb*

A PASSION FOR FRENCH POETRY

A bouquet of green holly and heather in flower.

  Until the last line of the penultimate stanza we think that all is well, although "le dos courbé" and particularly *"les mains croisées"* may have suggested prayer to us. We will all react differently to this poem. Is he playing a clever trick with something serious or is he hitting us with the realization that life has to go on, as he walks near Harfleur.

  No trick with the next poem,

À Villequier

>Maintenant que Paris, ses pavés et ses marbres,
>Et sa brume et ses toits sont bien loin de mes yeux;
>Maintenant que je suis sous les branches des arbres,
>Et que je puis songer à la bonté des cieux;
>
>Maintenant que du deuil qui m'a fait l'âme obscure
> Je sors, pâle et vainqueur,
>Et que je sens la paix de la grande nature
> Qui m'entre dans le coeur;
>
>Maintenant que je puis, assis au bord des ondes,
>Ému par ce superbe et tranquille horizon,
>Examiner en moi les vérités profondes
>Et regarder les fleurs qui sont dans le gazon;
>
>Maintenant, ô mon Dieu! que j'ai ce calme sombre
> De pouvoir désormais
>Voir de mes yeux la pierre où je sais que dans l'ombre
> Elle dort pour jamais;
>
>Je viens à vous, Seigneur, père auquel il faut croire,
> Je porte à vous, apaisé,
>Les morceaux de ce coeur tout plein de votre gloire
> Que vous avez brisé;

A PASSION FOR FRENCH POETRY

Je viens à vous, Seigneur! confessant que vous êtes
Bon, clément, indulgent et doux, ô Dieu vivant!
Je conviens que vous seul savez ce que vous faites,
Et que l'homme n'est rien qu'un jonc qui tremble au vent;

Je conviens à genoux que vous seul, père auguste,
Possédez l'infini, le réel, l'absolu;
Je conviens qu'il est bon, je conviens qu'il est juste
Que mon coeur ait saigné, puisque Dieu l'a voulu!

Seigneur, je reconnais que l'homme est en delire
    S'il ose murmurer;
Je cesse d'accuser, je cesse de maudire,
    Mais laissez-moi pleurer!

Voyez-vous, nos enfants nous sommes bien nécessaires,
Seigneur; quand on a vu dans sa vie, un matin,
Au milieu des ennuis, des peines, des misères,
Et de l'ombre que fait sur nous notre destin,

Apparaître un enfant, tête chère et sacrée,
    Petit être joyeux,
Si beau, qu'on a cru voir s'ouvrir à son entrée
    Une porte des cieux;

Quand on a vu, seize ans, de cet autre soi-même
Croître la grace aimable et la douce raison,
Lorsqu'on a reconnu.que cet enfant qu'on aime
Fait le jour dans notre âme et dans notre maison;

Que c'est la seule joie ici-bas qui persiste
    De tout ce qu'on rêva,
Considérez que c'est une chose bien triste
    De le voir qui s'en va!

Now that Paris, its paving stones and its marbles,
And its fog and roofs are really far from my eyes;

A PASSION FOR FRENCH POETRY

*Now that I am under tree branches
And that I can dream of the goodness of heaven;*

*Now that from the grief which made my soul gloomy
        I emerge, pale and victorious,
And that I feel the peace of the whole of nature
        Coming into my heart.*

*Now that I can, sitting on the edge of the waves,
Moved by this superb and peaceful horizon,
Examine in myself profound truths
And look at the flowers that grow in the turf;*

*Now, oh my God! that I have this sombre calm
        To be able in future to
See with my eyes the stone where I know that in the shade
        She sleeps for ever.*

*I come to you, Lord, father in whom one must believe,
        I bring to you, appeased,
The pieces of this heart full of your glory
        That you have broken.*

*I come to you,Lord, confessing that you are
Good, merciful, indulgent and kind, oh living God.
I acknowledge that you alone know what you are doing,
And that man is nothing but a reed trembling in the wind.*

*I acknowledge on my knees that you alone, august father,
Possess the infinite, the real, the absolute;
I acknowledge that it is good, I acknowledge that it is just
That my heart should have bled, since God wished it!*

*Lord, I recognize that man is out of his senses
        If he dares to murmur;
I stop accusing, I stop cursing,
        But let me weep!*

Prys Owen

A PASSION FOR FRENCH POETRY

You see, our children are really necessary to us,
Lord; when one has seen, in one's life, one morning,
In the midst of cares, pain, misery,
And the shadows which form all our destiny,

Appear a child, dear and sacred head,
            Little joyous being,
So beautiful, that one has imagined seeing as he enters
            The door of heaven opening;

When one has seen, sixteen years of one's other self
Grow in lovable grace and gentle reason,
When one has recognized that this child whom one loves
Brings light into our soul and into our home;

That it is the single joy down here which lasts
            Of all that one dreamed of
Consider that it is a really sad thing
            To see it go.

These are selected stanzas from a long poem. The first four stanzas of this moving poem begin with the word "NOW". It seems that he is recovering bravely from the loss of his daughter. But then the tone changes brutally: "I come to you, Lord, Father in whom one must believe". Why must? Because of faith? Then it becomes an accusation. He brings to God the heart which He has broken. Although confessing that God is good and kind, mankind is only a reed trembling in the wind, whose heart bleeds because God has wished it.

How does Hugo make the final line of each stanza so challenging? He varies the structure of the twelve syllable Alexandrine line. He breaks it in half with "que vous avez brisé". He uses a line break (caesura) "Man is only a reed/trembling in the wind" and "that my heart has bled/because God so wished". There is a line full of horror claiming that creation is a large wheel which cannot move without crushing someone. Man can only be allowed to

A PASSION FOR FRENCH POETRY

weep - "Je cesse d'accuser/ je cesse de maudire/ Mais laissez-moi pleurer."

There are so many questions for the reader to ask, faced with this long cry of despair. Is he really addressing God? These are words which are often addressed to priests in confession. They are the eternal question of the meaning of existence.

Booz Endormi

I used to say that this was my overall favourite in French lyric poetry. I've read more since then but I still maintain that the imagery in the last two stanzas is as good as anything I have read. This is another Bible story. It is, of course, in the Book of Ruth. If one were a cynic one would perhaps say that the marriage was arranged by Naomi because Ruth was a young widow and Boaz an elderly widower. But we will read it as a romantic love story – Boaz and Ruth were to be the forebears of Jesus.

The first fifteen stanzas tell us about Boaz who was "quoique riche, à la justice enclin". We see him asleep near his bushels of wheat and it is immediately a charming portrait of a handsome old master.

> Sa barbe était d'argent comme un ruisseau d'avril,
> Sa gerbe n'était point avare ni haineuse,
> Quand il voyait passer quelque pauvre glaineuse,
- Laissez tomber exprès des épis, disait-il.

His beard was silvery like a stream in spring, His harvesting was not at all miserly or full of hate. When he saw some poor gleaning girl passing by, "Let some ears of corn fall deliberately," he said.

When Hugo describes Boaz's clothing, he uses a figure of speech often found in comedy. "Vêtu de probité candide et de lin blanc." *Clothed in probity and white linen.* To those working for him,

A PASSION FOR FRENCH POETRY

the sight of wheat pouring from sacks was like money flowing from public fountains.

Et, toujours du côté des pauvres ruisselant,
Ses sacs de grains semblaient des fontaines publiques.

The ageing poet likes to compare the mature man favourably with the young man.

Booz était bon maître et fidèle parent;
Il était généreux, quoiqu'il fût économe;
Les femmes regardait Booz plus qu'un jeune homme,
Car le jeune homme est beau mais le vieillard est grand.

Le vieillard, qui revient vers la source première,
Entre aux jours éternels et sort des jours changeants;
Et l'on voit de la flamme aux yeux des jeunes gens,
Mais dans l'oeil du vieillard on voit la lumière.

Boaz was a good master and a faithful kinsman; he was generous but thrifty. Women looked at Boaz more than at a young man, because the young man is handsome but the old man is great. The old man is on his way back to where he originated, entering eternity and leaving behind days of change; one sees flame in the eyes the young, but in the eyes of the old man one sees the light of wisdom. Notice how the contrast is emphasized by the division of the twelve syllable line.

The new section is marked by the single word: "Donc." We know Boaz now and we can get on with the story. But in a very familiar story- telling style –"long, long ago…" "Et ceci se passait dans des temps très anciens." This also heralds a new part of the story, when the supernatural intervenes. From above, a dream came to Boaz. But the style is still cosy. And the dream went like this. "Et ce songe était tel, que Booz vit un chêne" From the oak -

Une race y montait comme une longue chaine;
Un roi chantait en bas, en haut mourait un dieu.

A PASSION FOR FRENCH POETRY

Again, the hemistiche emphasises Jesus.

"How can this be?" says Boaz. "I'm over eighty".
"Je n'ai pas de fils et je n'ai plus de femme.

Voilà longtemps que celle avec qui j'ai dormi,
Ô Seigneur! a quitté ma couche pour le vôtre;
Et nous sommes encore tout mêlés l'un à l'autre,
Elle à demi vivante, et moi mort à demi."

A touching picture of a man grieving for his dead wife. *We are still mingled, one with the other, because to me she is still half alive and I am half dead without her.* Read these lines aloud to yourself, emphasising where the caesura comes half way through each line.

"Une race naîtrait de moi! Comment le croire?
Comment se pourrait-il que j'eusse des enfants?
Quand on est jeune, on a des matins triomphants,
Le jour sort de la nuit comme d'une victoire."

Again a touch of a smile on the face of the poet. *A race born from me? How could I have children? When one is young, one has triumphant mornings. Day follows night like a victory.*

Le cèdre ne sent pas une rose à sa base,
Et lui ne sentait pas une femme à ses pieds.

The cedar does not feel a rose at its base and he did not sense a woman at his feet. Then the language becomes quite direct.

Pendait qu'il sommeillait, Ruth, une Moabite,
S'était couchée aux pieds de Booz, le sein nu.

But he did not know that she was there, and she did not know what God expected of her. We have appropriately an exotically romantic poetic accompaniment to the scene.

A PASSION FOR FRENCH POETRY

Un frais parfum sortait des touffes d'asphodèle;
Les souffles de la nuit flottaient sur Galgala.

A fresh perfume floated from the cluster of asphodel; the night breezes floated over Galgala. This is the local colour which was important to the Romantic poets, And we know that nature was also: "On était dans le mois où la nature est douce."

We come to the final stanzas which I so admire. But first the names of the two towns which emphasize the local colour. We know about Ur. Does Jérimadeth exist? Or did Hugo, knowing that this stanza is going to end with "Ruth se demandait", say to himself : "I want something biblical to rhyme with "dait". Je rime à dait. Ah! Jérimadeth!"

On a much more lyrical, poetic note, imagine how a simple peasant girl, lying in the field after a day working with her sickle, and now looking up at the bright starry night, would describe the crescent moon. It looks like a golden sickle. Some harvesting God, passing by, must have negligently thrown it into the field of the stars.

Tout reposait dans Ur et dans Jérimadeth;
Les astres émaillaient le ciel profond et sombre;
Le croissant fin et clair parmi ces fleurs de l'ombre
Brillait à l'occident, et Ruth se demandait,

Immobile, ouvrant l'oeil à moitié sous ses voiles,
Quel dieu, quel moissonneur de l'éternel été
Avait, en s'en allant, négligemment jeté
Cette faucille d'or dans le champ des étoiles . .

All was at rest in Ur and in Jerimadeth;
The stars dotted the deep sombre sky;
The fine, clear crescent among the flowers of the night
Shone in the west, and Ruth asked herself,

A PASSION FOR FRENCH POETRY

Motionless, eyes half open under her veils,
What God, what harvester of the eternal summer
Had, as he was passing by, casually thrown
That golden sickle into the field of the stars.

ALFRED DE MUSSET 1810 – 1857

Musset was born eighteen years after Hugo so he was the young man of the Cénacle group of Romantic poets. Yet even he, sometimes thought of as the wild, self centred youngster, had the respect for discipline and structure which all these poets displayed. *La Nuit de Mai* starts with the Muse trying to get the poet to compose a poem, She is a teasing young lady whom he knows well.

Poète, prends ton luth et me donne un baiser:
La fleur de l'églantier sent ses bourgeons s'éclore.
Le printemps naît ce soir; les vents vont s'embraser;
Et la bergeronette, en attendant l'aurore,
Aux premiers buissons verts commence à se poser;
Poète, prends ton luth et me donne un baiser..

It is a song, the final line of the muse's request repeating the first. It is about nature, the familiar theme of the Cénacle. The first hemistiche of the third line is memorable.

Poet, take up your lute and kiss me;
The wild rose flower can feel its buds bursting open.
Spring is born this evening; the winds are really sweltering;
And the wagtail, awaiting the break of dawn,
Is about to perch on the first green shrubs;
Poet, take up your lute and kiss me

The poet is reluctant. It is dark in the valley! The Muse urges him again to take up his lute. Nature is still there and he can be inspired by thinking of his beloved.

A PASSION FOR FRENCH POETRY

Ce soir, tout va fleurir; l'immortelle nature
Se remplit de parfums, d'amour et de murmure,
Comme le lit joyeux de deux jeunes époux.

The poet is still uninspired. He is alone. "Ô solitude! Ô pauvreté!"
But the Muse now chastises him: "Ô paresseux enfant! Regarde, je
suis belle. Notre premier baiser, ne t'en souviens - tu pas?"
Don't you remember our first kiss. Lazy child, look, I am beautiful.
She understands him well, as she understood the young Byron

Viens, tu souffres, ami. Quelque ennui solitaire
Te ronge; quelque chose a gémi dans ton coeur;

*Come here, you are suffering my friend, some solitary care
is consuming you* . The Muse takes over and we have her urging him
to try every poetic theme, in a loud and hectoring outburst.

"Partons, nous sommes seuls, l'univers est à nous.
Voici la verte Écosse et la brune Italie,
Et la Grèce, ma mère, où le miel est si doux".

*Let's be off, we are alone, the whole universe is ours. Here
is Scotland, so green, and Italy burnt brown and Greece, my mother,
where the honey is so sweet.* She is swept along swiftly with
enthusiastic enumeration.

Chanterons-nous l'espoir, la tristesse ou la joie?
Tremperons-nous de sang les bataillons d'acier?
Suspendrons-nous l'amant sur l'échelle de soie?
Jetterons-nous au vent l'écume du coursier?

*Shall we sing of hope, sadness and joy?
Shall we steep steel battalions in blood?
Shall we suspend the lover on a silken ladder?
Shall we hurl into the wind the lather of the war-horse?*

We feel that despite his occasional self pity, it all came
easily to this young man. It flowed. And yet he knew how beautiful

are the songs in a minor key. He reminds the reader of the legend of the pelican who has been unable to find food for her children and offers them her own flesh. The poet must do the same, not remaining coldly detached but offering his feelings, his soul to his readers. Instead of the seventeenth century call: *Je pense, donc je suis*, (Cogito ergo sum), we have *Je sens, donc je suis*.

- Les plus désespérés sont les chants les plus beaux,
- Et j'en sais d'immortels qui sont de purs sanglots.

The most desperate songs are the most beautiful and I know immortal ones which are the purest tears.

Lorsque le pélican, lassé d'un long voyage,
Dans les brouillards du soir retourne à ses roseaux,
Ses petits affamés courent sur le rivage.

Pêcheur mélancolique, il regarde les cieux.
Le sang coule à longs flots de sa poitrine ouverte;
En vain il a des mers fouillé la profondeur:
L'Océan était vide et la plage déserte;
Pour toute nourriture il apporte son coeur.

The poet must do likewise and melancholy must be a major theme.

THÉOPHILE GAUTIER 1811- 1872

Gautier was virtually the same age as Musset but he advocated a detachment on the part of the poet. Poetry is as difficult a medium as marble, onyx and enamel But once mastered it is long lasting. He expresses himself crisply in his poem *L'Art*.

Oui, l'oeuvre sort plus belle,
D'une forme au travail
Rebelle,

A PASSION FOR FRENCH POETRY

Vers, marbre, onyx, émail
Lutte avec le carrare,
Avec le paros dur
Et rare,
Gardiens du contour pur.

Peintre, fuis l'aquarelle,
Et fixe la couleur
Trop frêle
Au four de l'émailleur

Tout passe. L'art robuste
Seul à l'éternité
Le buste
Survit à la cité.

Les dieux eux-mêmes meurent,
Mais les vers souverains
Demeurent
Plus forts que les airains.

Sculpte, lime, cisèle ;
Que ton rêve flottant
Se scelle
Dans le bloc resistant.

Struggle with rare and hard marbles which guard pure contours. Painter, flee from watercolour, frail colour has to be toughened in the oven . Almost everything passes. Only robust art survives the city.

    It was not only in Pompey that this verse came back to me in all its strength. We were in the Languedoc, in a little village called Monestiés. Years ago someone digging deep in a garden came upon several statues of disciples holding and mourning their dead saviour. They are beautifully kept on display by the local folk. They are of stone but the grief and love on the faces live.

A PASSION FOR FRENCH POETRY

I was so aware of the contrast between what I saw in Monestiés and the things called "art" that were being displayed and sold in galleries in great cities, that I gathered my courage to write a sonnet about the issue. My words echo those of Gautier. This is just the last quatrain and the couplet.

> Not now the skilful craftsman at his trade
> Striving to capture on a canvas bare
> Beauty, before the Muse's urge does fade.
>
> Art's no quick gimmick nor an easy dare
> But medium modelled with a message rare.

However, enough on the theory of art. We will leave Gautier with two stanzas - teasing lines in a poem called *Chinoiserie* which are a delight when read aloud to friends at a party, particularly if the friends know the names of the ladies mentioned by some of the great writers.

> Ce n'est pas vous, non, madame, que j'aime
> Ni vous non plus, Juliette, ni vous,
> Ophélia, ni Béatrix, ni même
> Laure la blonde, avec ses grands yeux doux.
>
> Celle que j'aime, à present, est en Chine;
> Elle demeure avec ses vieux parents,
> Dans une tour de porcelaine fine.
> Au fleuve Jaune, où sont les cormorants.

I like the "à present". The answer is of course the fine blue tower. She is on the lovely Willow Pattern porcelain.

Read for yourself from the Oxford Book of French Verse this artist's play with *Symphonie en Blanc Majeur*. I give you a taste of the whiteness. The first stanza introduces the northern tales of the swans (les femmes-cygnes) on the Rhine. Then we have whiteness.

> Son sein, neige moulée en globe.

A PASSION FOR FRENCH POETRY

Contre les camélias blancs
Et le blanc satin de sa robe
Soutient des combats insolents.

Dans ces grandes batailles blanches,
Satins et fleurs ont le dessous,
Et, sans demander leurs revanches,
Jaunissent comme des jaloux

Sur les blancheurs de son épaule,
Paros au grain éblouissant,
Comme dans une nuit du pôle,
Un givre invisible descend.

Her breast, snow moulded into a globe, maintains an insolent combat against the white camellias and the white satin of her robe. In these great white battles, satins and flowers get the worst of it, and without asking for revenge, turn yellow as if jealous. On the whiteness of her shoulder, Paros with dazzling grain, an invisible hoar frost comes down, as in a polar night.

LECONTE DE LISLE 1818 – 1894

This poet's Saturday evening "at homes" in the eighteen sixties led to the establishment of the Parnassian school of French poetry. The stress was on moving away from the personal lyricism of Musset towards a celebration of beauty as the only aim of art.

I have chosen one of my especial favourites to illustrate the achievements of the Parnassians. I think that it always appeals to me because it reminds me of the life and works of another of my favourites - Antoine de Saint Exupéry from the twentieth century. He was one of the pioneering airmen who delivered mail across the vast expanses of deserts and particularly above the high Andes.

Le Sommeil du Condor

A PASSION FOR FRENCH POETRY

    Par delà l'escalier des roides Cordillères,
    Par delà les brouillards hantés des aigles noirs,
    Plus haut que les sommets creusés en entonnoirs
    Où bout le flux sanglant des laves familières,
    L'envergure pendante et rouges par endroits,
    Le vaste Oiseau tout plein d'une morne indolence,
    Regarde l'Amérique et l'espace en silence,
    Et le sombre soleil qui meurt dans ses yeux froids.
    La nuit roule de l'Est, où les pampas sauvages
    Sous les monts étagés s'élargissent sans fin;
    Elle endort le Chili, les villes, les rivages,
    Et la mer Pacifique et l'horizon divin;
    Du continent muet elle s'est emparée:
    Des sables aux coteaux, des gorges aux versants,
    De cime en cime, elle enfle, en tourbillons croissants,
    Le lourd débordement de sa haute marée.

All this is poured out in a huge flow of language. The final couplet takes the bird into space where he sleeps.

    Et, loin du globe noir, loin de l'astre vivant,
    Il dort dans l'air glacé, les ailes toutes grandes.

Beyond the stair of the steep Cordilleras, beyond the mists haunted by the black eagles, higher than the summits hollowed into craters where end the bleeding flow of the familiar lava, the wingspan pendant and in places red, the vast Bird, indolently bleak, looks at America and space in silence, and the sombre sun which dies in his cold eyes. The night rolls in from the East, where the savage pampas under the tiered mountains spreads unending. Putting Chile to sleep, the towns and the shores, and the Pacific ocean and the divine horizon; it has taken hold of the silent continent: from the sands to the slopes, the gorges and hillsides, from peak to peak , it swells, in crossing whirlwinds the heavy overflow of its high tide.

A PASSION FOR FRENCH POETRY

The last two lines capture the Condor's distant detachment from everything.

Et, loin du globe noir, loin de l'astre vivant,
Il dort dans l'air glacé, les ailes toutes grandes.

CHARLES BAUDELAIRE 1821- 1867

I recommend that you try to buy, beg or borrow a copy of *Baudelaire. Sartre and Camus* by Professor Garnet Rees, University of Wales Press, 1976. It is still in print. You will find a wonderful introduction to the poetry, and a commentary on one of Baudelaire's greatest poems, *Le Cygne*. I can only claim that it would not have been written had I not said to my former colleague W Eirwyn Thomas HMI : "We have run several one week courses on using audio-visual aids to teach languages in the lower school. Now I want to refresh sixth form teachers and myself by running such an HMI course on teaching French literature in the sixth form." Eirwyn responded that Professor Garnet Rees of Hull University would be an excellent specialist colleague. I was given authority to run such a course if a minimum of forty teachers applied to come for a week during their summer holiday. We received over a hundred applications and ran two courses – the first in September 1971 and the second the following Easter. Both were held in University College, Bangor. At the end of the second I said to Garnet that the reponse from teachers was so enthusiastic that his lectures and commentaries should be published. Eirwyn volunteered to contact the University of Wales Press. The book appeared in 1976. Garnet had been busy with his work on Appollinaire and modestly wrote on our book: "To Prys, this exercise in pedagogy with all good wishes, Garnet." Eirwyn suggested that the next course should be held in France, at Marly le Roi. I was still involved in at least one more of these courses but I was then moved over from languages to responsibility for teacher training in Wales. Eirwyn took the Marly courses to another level by arranging for French teachers to join

A PASSION FOR FRENCH POETRY

their colleagues from England and Wales and for the French dramatist Eugène Ionesco to join Garnet as visiting lecturer. With the permission of the Senior Chief Inspector Sheila Brown, two English HMIs join the staff Brian Arthur and Joe Trickey. My last memory of Marly was acting the part of the huge headmaster who killed his pupil (a tiny lady member of the course) in our Welsh translation of Ionesco's drama. Ionesco was delighted.

So I will not attempt to introduce Baudelaire's great poem *Le Cygne* except to say that as soon as they read the first line: "Andromaque, je pense à vous", and saw the dedication to Victor Hugo, exiled to the Channel Islands, educated French people would know that the swan struggling in the dust of a Paris building site was also a symbol of exile.

Baudelaire's sonnet *Correspondences* was a key statement for the Symbolist poets.

> La nature est un temple où de vivants piliers
> Laissent parfois sortir de confuses paroles;
> L'homme y passe à travers des forêts de symboles
> Qui l'observent avec des regards familiers.

This is far from the nature of Lamartine's *Le Lac*. The pillars of nature's temple are living things, sending us mysterious messages and the forest of symbols are looking at us. There is a vast unity, dark yet clear, where perfumes, colours and sounds mingle and correspond to each other. After introducing this mysterious, other reality in the quatrains Baudelaire enlarges on what he has to say about perfumes. Some are fresh like the skin of children, soft like the sound of oboes, green like prairies, others are corrupt and triumphant like amber, musk, Benjamin (a gum resin from Sumatra used for ointments and perfume), incense, "singing the transports of the spirit and the senses."

> Comme de longs échos qui de loin se confondent
> Dans une ténébreuse et profonde unité,
> Vaste comme la nuit et comme la clarté,

A PASSION FOR FRENCH POETRY

Les parfums, les couleurs et les sons se répandent.

Il est des parfums frais comme des chairs d'enfants,
Doux comme les hautbois, verts comme les prairies,
-Et d'autres, corrompus, riches et triomphants.

My two other poems by Baudelaire are less mysterious.

L' Invitation au Voyage

    Mon enfant, ma soeur,
    Songe à la douceur
D'aller là-bas vivre ensemble!
    Aimer à loisir,
    Aimer et mourir
Au pays qui te ressemble!
    Les soleils mouillés
    De ces ciels brouillés
Pour mon esprit ont les charmes
    Si mystérieux
    De tes traîtres yeux,
Brillant à travers leurs larmes.

Là, tout n'est qu'ordre et beauté,
Luxe, calme et volupté.

    Des meubles luisants,
    Polis par les ans,
Décoreraient notre chambre;
    Les plus rares fleurs
    Mêlant leurs odeurs
Aux vagues senteurs de l'ambre,
    Les riches plafonds,
    Les miroirs profonds,
    La splendeur orientale,

A PASSION FOR FRENCH POETRY

    Tout y parlerait,

À l'âme en secret
 Sa douce langue natale.

   Là tout n'est qu'ordre et beauté,
   Luxe, calme et volupté.

    Vois sur ces canaux
    Dormir ces vaisseaux
Dont l'humeur est vagabonde;
     C'est pour assouvir
     Ton moindre désir
Qu'ils viennent du bout du monde.
    -Les soleils couchants
     Revêtent les champs,
Les canaux, la ville entière,
     D'hyacinthe et d'or;
     Le monde s'endort
Dans une chaude lumière.

   Là, tout n'est qu'ordre et beauté,
   Luxe, calme et volupté.

    Short lines like the ones we will meet in Verlaine, and the same music. There is the uncertainty of whether this is a lover or someone who pleases with the qualities of a child or sister. There is also the use of the adjective "traîtres" to describe her eyes. Once again we have a poem which should be simply read aloud for its sounds and rhythms without translation. It is enough to think of the pleasure of going over there together to the country which is just like you. *The misty suns of your blurred skies have the same mysterious charm for me as the deceiving eyes shining through your tears.* What is it all about? Order and beauty throughout, with luxury, calm and pleasure. And this is the vital couplet repeated twice more in the poem. Baudelaire keeps to the linguistic and structural traditions of French lyric poetry.

A PASSION FOR FRENCH POETRY

We move on from his companion to the places where they will stay. *Shining furniture polished by the years will decorate our room. The rarest flowers, mingling their odours to the vague scent of amber, the rich ceilings, the deep mirrors, the oriental splendour, everything there would (if you accept the invitation) speak to the soul secretly in its sweet native tongue.* I have to keep repeating: "You know the meaning now, listen to the sounds. Listen to the vowels, listen to the rhymes. Say them, whisper them, declaim them." *Luisant* and *ans, fleurs* and *odeurs, chambre* and *ambre, plafonds* and *profonds, orientale* and *natale.* Is she back home after all in her native land? *Order, beauty, luxury, calm and voluptuousness .*

Everything combines now to satisfy her slightest wish. *See on these canals, vessels dozing in a vagabond mood. It is from the end of the world that they come to satisfy your slightest wish. The setting suns re-clothe the fields, the canals, the whole town in hyacinth and gold: the whole world falls asleep in a warm glow.*

There, everything is only order and beauty, luxury, calm and ecstasy.

Recueillement

>Sois sage, ô ma Douleur, et tiens-toi plus tranquille,
>Tu réclamais le Soir; il descend; le voici;
>Une atmosphère obscure enveloppe la ville,
>Aux uns portant la paix, aux autres le souci.
>Pendant que des mortels la multitude vile,
>Sous le fouet du Plaisir, ce bourreau sans merci,
>Va cueillir des remords dans la fête servile,
>Ma Douleur, donne-moi la main; viens par ici,
>Loin d'eux. Vois se pencher les défuntes Années,
>Sur les balcons du ciel, en robes surannées;
>Surgir du fond des eaux le Regret souriant;
>Le Soleil moribond s'endormir sous une arche,
>Et, comme un long linceul trainant à l'Orient,
>Entends ma chère, entends la douce Nuit qui marche.

A PASSION FOR FRENCH POETRY

This, like *Correspondences*, is a Petrarchan sonnet, two quatrains and two tercets, which contrasts with the Shakespearean sonnet of three quatrains and a couplet.

Meditation, contemplation. The poet is speaking to a friend who is very familiar to Romantic poets - sorrow, suffering. *Be good and be more tranquil. You craved the Evening; it falls, here it is; a dark atmosphere envelops the town, to some bringing peace, to others cares.* The poet now separates them from the vile multitude of mortals who, under the whip of Pleasure, that merciless hangman, gather remorse in the servile town. *While they do this, My Grief, give me your hand, come here far from them."* Note the powerful effect of this *enjambement* - separating them off. "Loin d'eux" on its own at the beginning of the line with a full stop.

What will they see together? We are now swept in the imagination, which is so vital to this poet, to a view of Years Gone By, *leaning over the balconies of the sky, clothed in dated robes, and, with a smile, surging, from the depth of the waters. They will also see the moribund sun, at death's door, sleeping under* an arch, *and like a long shroud trailing to the East, listen, my dear, harken to the sweet Night walking by.*

You must read it aloud. It's great stuff! Especially the last two lines. We have the simile of the dying sun and the "long linceul", lengthening with the alliterative two letters *l* the Night passing by. Most of all, feel the wonderful rhythm of the last line.

PAUL VERLAINE   1844 –1896

I have already compared the music in Baudelaire's poetry with what we find throughout Verlaine's. When we come to his *Art Poetique* we will hear the key words –"de la musique encore et toujours". But that will come after the other Verlaine poems which I have chosen.

A PASSION FOR FRENCH POETRY

His music is not the dramatic Beethoven which I like to play when I read about the retreat from Moscow, and it is worth contrasting Hugo's colourful sunsets with Verlaine's *Soleils Couchants*. But I will start with *Chanson d'Automne.* Instead of beginning with a description of coloured leaves - the blazing reds of New England or the browns and yellows of France - Verlaine begins with the impact of the season on his heart, and the music which goes with it. I asked our music specialist what music I could play as I read aloud "Les sanglots longs des violons de l'automne blessent mon coeur d'une langueur monotone." Instead of replying by letter he sent me an extract from Bruch's violin concerto. Try it. Of course, that single sentence is also the whole six line first stanza. Remember this when you read *Le Pont Mirabeau* by Appollinaire. No full stops there.

> Les sanglots longs
> Des violons
>   De l'automne
> Blessent mon coeur
> D'une langueur
> Monotone.
>
> Tout suffoquant
> Et blême, quand
> Sonne l'heure,
> Je me souviens
> Des jours anciens
> Et je pleure.
>
> Et je m'en vais
> Au vent mauvais
> Qui m'emporte
> De çà, de là,
> Pareil à la
> Feuille morte.

Prys Owen

A PASSION FOR FRENCH POETRY

Pale, and choking, when the hour strikes, I remember days gone by and I weep. And I go on my way in the harsh wind which carries me off, hither and thither, like the dead leaf.

It is only in the last three lines that Verlaine mentions autumn leaves using a beautiful simile. We have all seen how autumn leaves fall . Otherwise, it is all about the impression that the season leaves on the poet. We have "blessent mon coeur, je me souviens, je pleure, je m'en vais qui m'emporte." An impression conveyed by the musicality of short lines and those long vowels – *sanglots, longs, violons, automne, mon coeur, monotone, tout suffoquant.*

When he eventually says: "De ça, de là," we wonder how he is going to rhyme with the last syllable. It is the daring "Pareil à la…" I love it.

Quite different but equally enchanting are *Mon Rêve Familier* and *Colloque Sentimental*. The first will help us to answer a question which comes to mind as we read the second.

Je fais souvent ce rêve étrange et pénétrant,
D'une femme inconnue, et que j'aime, et qui m'aime
Et qui n'est, chaque fois, ni tout à fait la même
Ni tout à fait une autre, et m'aime et me comprend.

Car elle me comprend, et mon coeur, transparent
Pour elle seule, hélas! cesse d'être un problème
Pour elle seule, et les moîteurs de mon front blême
Elle seule les sait rafraichir, en pleurant.

Est-elle brune, blonde ou rousse? - Je l'ignore.
Son nom? Je me souviens qu'il est doux et sonore,
Comme ceux des aimés que la Vie exila.

Son regard est pareil au regard des statues,
Et pour sa voix, lointaine, et calme, et grave, elle a

A PASSION FOR FRENCH POETRY

L'inflexion des voix chères qui se sont tues.

We are back with the traditional sonnet, though here also we have the daring rhyme – *exila* and *elle a*. Although the structural rules of the sonnet are tight we are not in what Wordsworth calls "the convent's narrow room".

In sundry moods, 'twas pastime to be bound
Within the Sonnet's scanty plot of ground;
Pleased if some Souls (for such there needs must be)
Who have felt the weight of too much liberty,
Should find brief solace there, as I have found.
(from *Nuns fret not at their convent's narrow room*).

Verlaine would have loved the words "pastime" and "solace" to describe the poet's pleasure when things go well.

The poet has a frequently recurrent dream of an unknown woman whom he loves and who loves him and who understands him. He immediately starts the second quatrain by reiterating the end of the first."Car elle me comprend". Repetition is used again. *Transparent for her alone* is the beginning of the second and third lines of the second quatrain. And she alone is able to refresh his troubled face with her tears.

The tercets begin on an almost playful note. Is she brunette, blond or red haired? I've no idea. Her name? Sweet and sonorous. But then the mood changes back to sadness in the simile: like that of loved ones whom Life has exiled. Her glance is like that of a statue, and her voice is distant, calm and grave. The poem makes us catch our breath with its ending. First we have the penultimate line ending with "elle a" to rhyme with "exila" in the first tercet and then the *enjambement* leading to the most touching line in the poem . Read it to yourself quietly for the last four words. *The inflection of dear voices which are now silent.*

Colloque sentimental

A PASSION FOR FRENCH POETRY

This poem is the last one in the collection *Fêtes Galantes* which you will not understand unless you first look at some paintings by Watteau. The first poem in this collection is *Clair de Lune* and its first stanza sets the scene.

> Votre âme est un paysage choisi
> Que vont charmants masques et bergamasques,
> Jouant du luth et dansant et quasi
> Tristes sous leurs déguisements fantasques.

Colloque Sentimental

> *In the old solitary frozen park, two forms passed by just now. Their eyes are dead and their lips are limp and their voices can barely be heard. In the old, solitary, frozen park two spectres evoked the past. "Do you remember our former ecstasy?" "So why do you want me to remember?" "Does your heart still beat faster just at the very sound of my name? Do you still see my soul in a dream?" - "No." "Ah! The beautiful days of indescribable happiness when we joined our lips!" "It's possible." "How blue the sky was and hope was great." "Hope has fled, defeated, to the black sky."*

Three couplets set the scene in this little play. The third couplet echoes the first, as in a song, only changing from "forme" to "spectre," Then we have the sad regret of one person and the cold rejection by the other. You need three actors to bring this alive for you, probably a friend to set the scene and a man to be the sad lover and a woman to coldly reject.

> Dans le vieux parc solitaire et glacé
> Deux formes ont tout à l'heure passé.
>
> Leurs yeux sont morts et leurs lèvres sont molles,
> Et l'on entend à peine leurs paroles.
>
> Dans le vieux parc solitaire et glacé
> Deux spectres ont evoqué le passé..

Prys Owen

A PASSION FOR FRENCH POETRY

- Te souvient-il de notre extase ancienne?
- Pourquoi voulez-vous donc qu'il m'en souvienne?

- Ton coeur bat-il toujours à mon seul nom?
Toujours vois-tu mon âme en rêve? - Non.

- Ah! Les beaux jours de bonheur indicible
Où nous joignions nos bouches! -C'est possible.

- Qu'il était beau, le ciel, et grand, l'espoir!
- L'espoir a fui, vaincu, vers le ciel noir.

Tels ils marchaient dans les avoines folles,
Et la nuit seule entendit leurs paroles.

Did you notice that one character used the tu form and the other the vous?

I have very happy professional memories of introducing the next poem to my pupils, *Le ciel est par-dessus le toit*. Like many of Verlaine's poems, it looks deceptively simple. I read it slowly like a story to my group of sixth formers. When I got to the first line of the fourth and last little stanza, one of the not always responsive young men suddenly exclaimed : "Mon Dieu, he's in prison - it could be Jack speaking!" It was no longer a nineteenth century French poet who was involved, but a friend.

Le ciel est, par-dessus le toit,
    Si bleu, si calme!
Un arbre, par-dessus le toit,
    Berce sa palme.

La cloche dans le ciel qu'on voit
    Doucement tinte,
Un oiseau sur l'arbre qu'on voit
    Chante sa plainte.

A PASSION FOR FRENCH POETRY

Mon Dieu, mon Dieu, la vie est là
    Simple et tranquille,
Cette paisible rumeur-là
    Vient de la ville.

-Qu'as-tu fait, ô toi que voilà
    Pleurant sans cesse,
Dis, qu'as-tu fait, toi que voilà,
    De ta jeunesse?

    I'm not going to translate this. He's looking through prison bars at the simple peaceful things of life. What have you done with your life? Note the musical repetition of the rhymes – *toit toi, calme, palme* and then *voit, voit* and *tinte, plainte, là, là, tranquille, ville,* finally *voilà, voilà,* and *cesse, jeunesse*.

Art poétique

    There are seven stanzas in this poem. Some are technical – "pour cela préfère l'impair" (uneven number of syllables in a line); rhyme which is worth only a farthing, and deliberately making a daring rhyme of *cou* and *jusq'où* (we've seen Verlaine creating several daring rhymes). To whom is he speaking? "Il faut que tu n'ailles point" (you absolutely must not go) and the tu form "tes mots". A young would-be poet perhaps. And yet we pick up what he considers essential, Music above all, nothing slow and heavy, a balance between indecisive and precise, lovely eyes but half hidden by a veil, a warm autumn evening with starry skies, only a hint of colour, a nuance which blends the dream to the dream and the flute to the horn. Not sarcasm and impure laughter which are like the garlic of low quality cooking. Music again and always, so that your verse is a soul in flight towards other skies and other loves. Listen to the last stanza and you have the glory of Verlaine.

    Que ton vers soit la bonne aventure
    Éparse au vent crispé du matin
    Qui va fleurant la menthe et le thym....

A PASSION FOR FRENCH POETRY

Et tout le reste est littérature.

It's as though he's telling a musician how to compose like Mozart. He's certainly telling people like me that we are doing mere literature. Let us just recall a couple more stanzas but read the whole poem yourself.

> C'est de beaux yeux derrière des voiles
> C'est le grand jour tremblant de midi,
> C'est par un ciel d'automne attiédi
> Le bleu fouillis des claires étoiles!
>
> Car nous voulons la Nuance encore,
> Pas la couleur, rien que la Nuance!
> Oh! La nuance seule fiance
> Le rêve au rêve et la flute au cor!

This is Impressionism, just like the painters.

JEAN-ARTHUR RIMBAUD 1854 – 1891

Rimbaud wrote his poetry between the ages of sixteen and twenty one. He was the young rebel, yet he saw Baudelaire as his master. He used a range of poetic forms and he reacted vigorously both to the enjoyment of life and to its horrors. The three poems which I have chosen amply illustrate this.

Ma Bohème concerns a young lad savouring the freedom of the open road and the glory of being the Muse's faithful follower. *Les Effarés* is a Dickens-like picture of poverty - starving, cold children looking at the Baker at his hot oven. I have already compared *Le Dormeur du Val* with one of Hugo's masterpieces. As you get more confident, read *Voyelles* and think of Baudelaire. Then *Le Bateau Ivre*. Why did this genius give up poetry and go gun running?

A PASSION FOR FRENCH POETRY

Ma Bohème

    Je m'en allais, les poings dans mes poches crevées;
    Mon paletot aussi devenait idéal ;
    J'allais sous le ciel, Muse! et j'étais ton féal;
    Oh! là, là! que d'amours splendides j'ai revées

    Mon unique culotte avait un large trou.
    - Petit-Poucet rêveur, j'égrenais dans ma course
    Des rimes. Mon auberge était à la Grande-Ourse.
    - Mes étoiles au ciel avaient un doux frou-frou

    Et je les écoutais, assis au bord des routes,
    Ces bons soirs de septembre où je sentais des gouttes
    De rosée à mon front, comme un vin de vigueur;

    Où, rimant au milieu des ombres fantastiques,
    Comme des lyres, je tirais les élastiques
    De mes souliers blessés, un pied près de mon coeur!

What a sonnet! Ronsard would have been proud of him.

I was on my way, my fists in my pockets full of holes
*My overcoat was also becoming ideal (*not much reality*)*
I went, the sky above me, Muse! I was your faithful
servant;
Oh la la! What splendid dreams I dreamed!

My only breeches had a big hole.
- Dreamy Tom Thumb, I rolled off on my trip
Rhymes. My inn was under the Great Bear
- My stars in the sky made a swishing show

And I listened to them, seated on the side of the roads,
Those good September evenings when I felt drops
Of dew on my temple, like a wine of vigour;

Prys Owen

A PASSION FOR FRENCH POETRY

Where, rhyming in the midst of fantastic shades,
Like lyres, I plucked the elastics
Of my wounded shoes, holding one foot close to my heart.

How wonderfully he conveys his sense of freedom, his confidence as a poet and the glorification of his ragged clothing. Finally, he combines the them all by making music, plucking the elastic holding up his tattered shoes, with one foot held close to his heart.

Les Effarés

But like many teenagers, he was shocked by seeing suffering children. He castigates these social evils, and yet I am using the wrong verb. He does not specifically curse society, but paints a picture of hunger and homelessness.

Black in the snow and in the fog,
At the big vent which gives some warmth to their round bums,
On their knees, five little ones - misery!

Look at the Baker making the sound white bread. The poet does not need a castigating verb. The word "misery", detached, alone, tells the whole story. Why a capital letter for the baker? The children watch and they listen. They see the strong arm turning the grey dough and thrusting it into a glowing hole. They listen to the good bread cooking. The Baker, with a fat smile grunts an old tune. Again the capital B. Is he just a human being or is he more than that, performing this miracle of the creation of daily bread?

They are huddled. Note that all the verbs are in the present tense. It is all happening now. Not one of them moves, by the breath of the red vent, warm as a breast. Here are the five first stanzas. Read them aloud, making sure that *misère* gets its proper emphasis and that the long vowel sounds of *le lourd pain blanc* are not rushed.

Noirs dans la neige et dans la brume,

A PASSION FOR FRENCH POETRY

Au grand soupirail qui s'allume,
    Leurs culs en rond,

À genoux, cinq petits - misère! -
Regardent le Boulanger faire
    Le lourd pain blanc
La pâte grise et qui l'enfourne
    Dans un trou clair.

Ils sont blottis, pas un ne bouge,
Au souffle du soupirail rouge
    Chaud comme un sein.

Quand pour quelque médianoche,
Façonné comme une brioche,
    On sort le pain,

Quand sous les poûtres enfumées
Chantent les croûtes parfumées
    Et les grillons,

Que ce grand trou chaud souffle la vie,
Ils ont leur âme si ravie
    Sous leurs haillons,

Ils se ressentent si bien vivre,
Les pauvres Jésus pleins de givre,
    Qu'ils sont là tous,

Collant leurs petits museaux roses
Au treillage, grognant des choses
    Entre les trous,

Tout bêtes, faisant leurs prières
Et repliés vers ces lumières
    Du ciel rouvert,

Si fort, qu'ils crèvent leur culotte

Prys Owen

A PASSION FOR FRENCH POETRY

> Et que leur chemise tremblote
> Au vent d'hiver.

When I was in college the rooms of our hall of residence were over a bakery. We worked into the early hours and took it in turns to go down to get *le bon pain blanc*. But we had the money to buy it and we were not cold. These children are pressed against the grill and the vent is warm as a breast.

From now on there is no full stop for the last seven stanzas. Two now begin with "quand". *When for some midnight feast, the bread comes out, in the shape of a brioche*. The poet gives "On sort le pain" extra emphasis by its position. *When under the smoking beams the perfumed crusts and the crickets are singing*. (Again the reversal.) I'm reminded of Baudelaire when all these senses (the perfumes, the sounds and the warmth) combine to form one unity.

This warm hole gives forth the breath of life (can you hear the Bible?) Their soul is so delighted, under their rags, that they feel that it's good to be alive, the little Jesuses, frozen stiff, who are all there together, sticking their little pink snouts to the grill, grunting things between the gaps. They are not saying human words but are just grunting - "tout bêtes", like animals, and yet "faisant leurs prières". Are these just animal urges or are these real prayers that they remember from somewhere, a home, a church, an institution? They are bending forward so tightly and eagerly towards the light and the sky that they split their breeches and their shirts flutter in the winter wind. Rimbaud has captured us so completely by this one continuous sentence that we are on the verge of tears, wondering what will happen to these little Jesus figures, becoming animals. Does someone say: "Let them come to me for of such is the Kingdom of Heaven"? But this extraordinary twenty year old does not let us off the hook with a Hollywood ending, He ends with the winter wind.

Dormeur du Val

Prys Owen

A PASSION FOR FRENCH POETRY

We will leave Rimbaud with another sonnet. But this not a wild celebration of bohemian escape. He describes a quiet idyllic countryside scene, "un val qui mousse de rayons", a valley frothing with sunbeams.

>C'est un trou de verdure où chante une rivière
>Accrochant follement aux herbes des haillons
>D'argent; où le soleil, de la montagne fière,
>Luit: c'est un petit val qui mousse de rayons.
>
>Un soldat jeune, bouche ouverte, tête nue,
>La nuque baignant dans le frais cresson bleu,
>Dort; il est étendu dans l'herbe, sous la nue,
>Pâle dans son lit vert où la lumière pleut.
>
>Les pieds dans les glaieuls, il dort. Souriant comme
>Sourirait un enfant malade, il fait un somme:
>Nature, berce-le doucement: il a froid.
>
>Les parfums ne font pas frissonner sa narine;
>Il dort dans le soleil, la main sur la poitrine
>Tranquille. Il a deux trous rouges au côté droit.

It is a verdant little spot where a river is singing and hanging extravagantly silver rags on the grasses; where the sun, from the proud mountain, shines forth: it is a valley frothing with sunbeams.

A young soldier, open mouthed, head bare, and the nape of his neck bathed in the fresh water cress, sleeps; he is stretched out on the grass, under the cloud, pale in his green bed where the light rains down. His feet in the sword-lilies, he sleeps. Smiling as a sick child would smile, he's taking a nap. Nature, nurse him warmly, he's cold. The perfumes do not make his nostrils quiver; he is sleeping in the sun, his hand on his breast, at peace. He has two red holes in his right side.

A PASSION FOR FRENCH POETRY

I told you that this reminds me of Victor Hugo's *Demain dès l'Aube* when it seems that the man is hurrying to meet his love, knowing that she will be waiting eagerly to see him. It is only at the end of the last stanza that we are told that he has a wreath of green holly and heather in flower to place on the grave of his daughter.

Here we see that our young bohemian has a complaint to lay before us. The 1870 war has claimed another victim. Rimbaud deliberately shocks us. His little animal Jesus children are cold and hungry, and now this young soldier is lying in the warm sun - not asleep, but dead. Note the positions of d*'argent, luit , dort and tranquille*. Note also the *enjambement* stressing "tranquille" in the last line contrasting with "trou rouge" Sorry - my mere literature!

GUILLAUME APPOLLINAIRE 1880 – 1918

We started with a soldier who fought at Agincourt in 1415 and we close with one who died in Flanders where my own father was gassed.

Le Pont Mirabeau

>Sous le pont Mirabeau coule la Seine
>	Et nos amours
>Faut-il qu'il m'en souvienne
>La joie venait toujours après la peine
>
>		Vienne la nuit sonne l'heure
>		Les jours s'en vont je demeure
>
>Les mains dans les mains restons face à face
>	Tandis que sous
>Le pont de nos bras passe
>Des éternels regards l'onde si lasse

A PASSION FOR FRENCH POETRY

       Vienne la nuit sonne l'heure
       Les jours s'en vont je demeure

L'amour s'en va comme cette eau courante
       L'amour s'en va
Comme la vie est lente
Et comme l'espérance est violente

       Vienne la nuit sonne l'heure
       Les jours s'en vont je demeure

Passent les jours et passent les semaines
       Ni temps passé
       Ni les amours reviennent
Sous le pont Mirabeau coule la Seine
       Vienne la nuit sonne l'heure
       Les jours s'en vont je demeure

Under the Mirabeau bridge flows the Seine and our loves must I remember The joy always comes after the pain Comes the night sounds the hour the days go by I remain Hands in hands let's stay face to face while under the bridge of our arms pass the so weary wave of eternal gazes Love goes by like running water Love goes by How slow life is And how violent is Hope Pass the days and pass the weeks Neither time past nor loves return

………………………………

A Post Scriptum bonus, by whom?

La lune blanche
Luit dans les bois;
De chaque branche
Part une voix
Sous la ramée -

Ô bien aimée

Prys Owen

A PASSION FOR FRENCH POETRY

L'étang reflète,
Profond miroir,
La silhouette
Du saule noir
Où le vent pleure.

Rêvons, c'est l'heure

Un vaste et tendre
Apaisement
Semble descendre
Du firmament
Que l'astre irise -

C'est l'heure exquise.

ACKNOWLEDGEMENTS

A PASSION FOR FRENCH POETRY

À mes amis français, leur langue et leur littérature.
2015 - Courage!

To my wife Reverend Susan Owen, M.A. St. Andrews, B.D., M.Phil. Wales, and Scottish lacrosse international (!) for critical editing and love.

To Chris Crook, Beddgelert, for permission to use one of his photographs on the cover.

ABOUT THE AUTHOR

A PASSION FOR FRENCH POETRY

Dr Prys Owen was an Education Officer in the Royal Air Force. He taught French in Latymer Upper School, in Regent Street Polytechnic, and King Henry VIII Grammar School, Abergavenny. He trained teachers at the University of Leeds and was Dean of Studies in Trinity College, Carmarthen. As an HMI in Wales he inspected French teaching and was responsible for teacher training.

Printed in Great Britain
by Amazon